The Loving
Selected Poems

Praise for *The Loving*

"It is an honor to read Rena Gerhard's poems, to touch in after decades with her precision of imagination and her encounters with daily life, laced with the generosity and intimacy of a 'trembling heart.' I love how Gerhard envisions herself standing 'at the door of a dark night' and whistling as 'the beautiful words come running.' Yet she also wrote herself through suffering. She recognized that she would have to 'look through the hollows between the words.' This memorial volume edited by her son, the poet Fred Gerhard, will stand as an enduring achievement."

—Heather H. Thomas, author of *Vortex Street* (FutureCycle Press, 2018) and former editor of *Musings,* poetry column, *Reading Eagle* newspaper

"Rena Gerhard weaves a tapestry of life's quiet wonders and profound depths, from the shimmering beauty of nature to the intimate struggles of the human spirit. This collection captures a lifelong love affair with words, faith, and family, inviting readers to dance through verses that resonate with emotional clarity and timeless grace."

—Peter David Orr, author of *Beneath the Surface of Shadow and Light* and *With the End in Mind*

"So many people long for that presence, which would keep their loved ones alive forever. We search under afghans, trapse through attics, and roam down long forgotten places for one gem, one picture, or one word that would help us remember. Rena, through her poetry, *The Loving* — she has remained. Be there for a moment with her, and soon, you too, will be jumping in and enjoying her enchanting dance with words."

—H. Alfke, author of *A Smattering: Life, Death, God, and Poetry*

"As the middle of the Twentieth Century approached, a young woman near Reading, Pennsylvania, took up poetry keenly aware of the thick, heavy glass ceiling hovering over every line she wrote. But write she did, and one could sense in the lines from her poem 'Night Walk':

> *Living through my night walk*
> *She's sleeping standing up ....*

Or in 'Midnight Forest':

> *The silence seems too tense.*
> *One fears to breathe in case one might*
> *Thus doing, cause offense.*

that she felt it deeply, but that she also saw cracks in the male ceiling already present, cracks that by the 1960s would demolish it, at least in poetry, and provide space for women equally at the forefront of our poets. And though she may not have publicly joined that movement, she quietly kept at it, quietly riding that horse, as she notes in 'Strange Steed':

> *When the wise had gone to bed*
> *To receive their well-earned rest,*
> *Then I watched him as he fed,*
> *And I sat his back, a guest*
> *Instead."*

—Rodger Martin, author of *The Sleeping Dogs of Lubec, The Nemo Poems: A Martian Perspective, The Blue Moon Series,* and *For All the Tea in Zhōngguó*

The Loving
Selected Poems

Rena Gerhard

Petronella Press

The Loving: Selected Poems
Rena Gerhard
© 2025 Fred Gerhard

Petronella Press, 8 Lawrence Street, Ashburnham, MA 01430.

ISBN: 979-8-9998858-1-4

Cover photograph by Florence and Robert Johnson

Author photograph by J. Calvin Gerhard

CONTENTS

Foreword

As a child I remember my mother, Rena Gerhard, reading poems to me like Edward Lear's "The Owl and the Pussy Cat." And later she encouraged me to read poems like Tennyson's "The Charge of the Light Brigade," Coleridge's "The Rime of the Ancient Mariner," and the ancient poem "Beowulf," and many others. She introduced the Bible to me through reading the Psalms of David. Even spiritual life had a door that was poetry. Her love for poetry was infectious and consequently I grew up really loving poems.

She was raised in Pottsville, Pennsylvania, where her father was a shoes salesman, and her mother a clinical psychologist. She recounted, in a small handwritten memoir, that her favorite poems were A. E. Houseman's "When I Was One-and-Twenty," Sir Walter Scott's "Lochinvar," Shelley's "Ozymandias," and Edna St. Vincent Millay's "The Dream" from *Renascence*. Other poets she loved included Rudyard Kipling, Sara Teasdale, Emily Dickinson, Robert Browning, Henry Wadsworth Longfellow, and John Keats.

She had collected her early poems into a notebook titled *Just Poems by Ethelrene Johnson*. She had told me that those were a child's poems, but also included her college poetry. Some of my favorites of these are the sonnet "Earth-Cry," "Jungle," and "Idyll." You will also get a glimpse into her perspective and growth as a young poet in "Poem to Old Writings" where she lets go of language that felt old-fashioned:

> *I shall be that of me*
> *Again! I shall be me.*
>
> *No longer old & rut-deep*
> *Riding same and known —*

No more!

In the 1980s, when I began to get poems published in *Musings,* the poetry column in the local newspaper, *The Reading Eagle,* she began to write again and followed suit. Many of her poems were published from the 1980s through the first decade of the 21st century. There are some amazing poems here like "Oh Dear," "Night Walk," "Sudden Fright," "Reunion," and "Words." During the end of this period she was developing brain cancer, which required an operation and treatment. Following that ordeal she was given a year to live. Some of her struggles at that time are evident in poems like "Late."

I am moved to see, even in her later years, some stunningly great poems. Look at her facile use of language, economy of words, and emotional impact in poems like "The Beautiful Words," "Plea," and the "Short Poems."

My mother made notes about many of her poems. These are collected at the back of the book and give a glimpse of her life and thoughts about her writings.

I am grateful to my father, J. Calvin Gerhard, for giving me permission to publish my mom's work here. May her poems touch your heart and soul, and encourage you to join the dance presented to you, be it the dance of words, or actual dancing, as she says in "Dancers,"

> *So when will you join the dance?*
> *PLEASE — say you will join the dance!*

Fred C. Gerhard
July, 2025

Introduction

Dear Reader,

If you wish to envision your author, I was an only child who loved to read, later, to write.

In the late 1940s – early 1950s I gathered my early poetry. Some poems speak of loneliness, and one of poets' favorite subjects – unrequited love "Earth Cry."

Not represented here is the hack "commercial" work. In high school girls would come to me in study hall to ask for a poem about them and their current heartthrob, and I'd link their names in a few lines predicting a rosy future for them. Whereupon I'd become ten cents richer and the girls would go off clutching my words, to moon over their crushes. (Fortunately, no copies are extant).

I imagine all poets start by noticing how pleasant rhyme and rhythm are. Then it becomes a game. A poem may spring from a feeling, a theological idea or something as simple as noticing "hey, that rhymes!" *I'll bet* even Shakespeare sat tapping his teeth with his quill while he took the ending of a word and tried each letter of the alphabet in front of it.

Ethel Irene Gerhard
December 2005

The Loving
Selected Poems

THE LOVING

Diamond-flashing, opal-gleamed —
    Mothers' loving shines
    Strong in those years of dust-disturbing
    Sandal prints where sons met foes
    and daughters' hot tears rained on folded clothing
Yet most in peace-bestowing, blessing-counting
    dream-beseeching
    prayers that climb her steepled hands
    while teaching, always teaching
    sons and daughters
    Mothers' mothers' mothers'
    dazzled awe
    at Heaven's Love
    and Love's bright call.

EARTH-CRY

Far vacillating star who makes
A shining and a bitter glow,
A shimmering song in vacuum lakes,
A crystal mace, a chill blue flow,
Give audience to a breath of dust
Nor sheathe yourself in centuries.
Why fascinate a mortal just?
Why make it feel such strange unease —
Let fatal glance—too cherished—strike
A stinging love—too deep for it.
Why cherish thus, all human-like,
A glance, O creature sadly smit,
While knowledge burdens every hour
That only planets charm a star?

BEAUTY

Tall and stately
Slender yet graceful
Quite sedately
Walk the sorrowful

Color and brightness
Lines and laughter
Join the lightness
For the master

Calm and stillness
Restful sea-scene
Th'elusive movement unceasing
Of a waveling

PERCEPTION

There isn't another feeling like
Being one small human
When there's a too-white seashell
There in the Sky
And music in your ears, so very gold
It's almost Red.
It isn't fair — yet, incredibly,
A man is big enough to hold the
Light with those two tiny
Cups called Eyes,
And then there's just enough of him
Left over to catch the music.

NIGHT WALK

All day
Maples shatter sun
to ruby, cat's eye yellow; gold.
Prismed vision —
What a way to meet our nearest star!

Living through my night walk
She's sleeping standing up
Having dreamed her children
to the wind —
Now verging on
Relinquishing lavish
Rough brown blankets crackling down
To mold, warm, live with
Microcosmic engines.

Queens in neat rows
Asleep on their feet
Yet nursing their babes
Most naturally.

ACCEPTING PEACE

'Neath hushed breathing
in the sepia evening,
Lavenders lap along the creeping
          indigo
and seep along gray limbs
of black, black walnuts

Behold the small gray gardener
blended to her branch,
her convex hammock.
Lids droop, oval; almond—
over tired black-liquid orbs,
ever, ever lower . . . finest slits.

The twilit squirrel stares,
faithful witness
to the down-slip of our common Star,
abruptly
knows she's done—
must turn
on slender graceful ankle
and glide, silent,
to her quiet nest.

THE WAVES

NPR on the car radio manifests
    in rising and falling cadences —
        a poem I can barely hear,
           perfectly mirrored in the
                undulating back of a black cat
           I can barely see.

His stalking makes a
    counterpoint to the
    universal swaying, April winds
    combing roadside grasses.

REUNION

Glistening white in merciless sun
A meeting of snails
Count back-streaks, seeking match.
Touched antennae retract . . .
          rehatch.

"Nice to see you again"
          sound catch, song-snatch . . .
Jig-cut memory, frayed to fuzz
          idly stirs cindered loves,
          rattles bones of dried fears—
By dinner, all glad
          of the armoring years.

Scarab-like they roll their fables,
     .   wistful of others' seemed eternity
All leave wrapped in china smiles
          to drop this newest pearl
          'midst treasures, truths and trials.

MIDNIGHT FOREST

Magic is afoot tonight,
The silence seems too tense.
One fears to breathe in case one might
Thus doing, cause offense.

That whispering sigh above your head,
Know you what it means?
A rustling leaf — long brown and dead
Or th' song of Fairy Queens.

The eerie shimmering rigid moon
Hostilely glides aloof.
As if the sun couldn't set too soon,
Plunging from the roof.

The challenging moon is overcome
By the Sovereign Call of the Wild.
That Call will never be heard by some.
They are deaf to its summons mild.

The frigid light of the conquered star
Cascades to the earth.
Where elfin playfellows dance a bar,
Then — Each to an elfin berth!

STRANGE STEED

When the dusk comes flowing in
Trailing shy stars at her heel,
When the blazoned sun has been,
And when nothing seems quite real,
Listen then.

When the world is done in grays
By the sky-pearl called the Moon,
And the lavish night arrays
Nocturnal wand'rers in her June,
He neighs!

When the wise had gone to bed
To receive their well-earned rest,
Then I watched him as he fed,
And I sat his back, a guest
Instead.

KING OF THE BEASTS

The horizon is touched with rose
The forest is taut with silence
Then through the stillness arose
The baby king's roar of defiance

The creatures lay back and smiled
The forest breathed freely again
The prince would be royally wild
A monarch throughout his domain

Those feathered began with their racket
And Thinkers took up meditation
And hunters came home from their banquet
All honored the princely creation

WEIRD WINTER

The cold, white, empty world
With stiff-necked starkness stares
The black trees, grotesquely gnarled,
Point at fear's home lairs.

The wild winds jeer at our attempts
To make friends with the cold.
They scream and mock like eerie imps
They marvel we withhold.

In abstract black and white — the cold
With hostile glittering eyes
Watches and waits to trip the old
With treacherous, crystal ice.

THIS SNOW

This snow I do not think we'll have to move
        but only love —
Heirloom lace spread perfectly smooth,
        the tablecloth land below
        meant to show!

Finest stitch of sparrow hops
        link bush to branch to porch to perch
While down white canyons —
        Last week's blizzard
                Laid aside awaiting thaws —
Squirrel-leap and rabbit dart
        basting stitch the path of paws.

All join in crochet whorls to ring
  the water
  And create star-ray leads
  approaching to the seeds.

LEFT-OVER DREAM

My couch was fragile floating leaf;
My sleep was mewing winds.
My storm-green nap was cool and sweet —
And wrapped in silky wings.

The musty, matted vines of thought
Were torn by stumbling dreams
That cut the chafing thongs of doubts
And sang in soothing drone.

And there were blade-tongued, rasp-limbed things
With terrible, silent tread,
And always eyes, white blinking ring,
Watched, reasonless, for death.

And then I wished a tree — I leapt
And touched rough, living bark.
I went too high, but then I laughed
In Afric slumber far.

Spring-warm half-timbered Tudor day —
Dear-cherished Ultimate.
I will not wake or let this fade —
Left-over dream centric!

EARTH-CRY (II)

Far vacillating star who has
A shining and a bitter glow,
A shimmering song in vacuum lakes,
A crystal mace, a flow of blue,
Give audience to a breath of dust
Nor sheathe yourself in centuries.
Why fascinate a mortal just?
Why make it feel such strangeness rise —
Let fatal glance — too cherished — strike
A stinging love — too deep for it?
Why cherish thus, in human streak,
A glance, O creature smitten yet
While knowledge burdens every hour
This spell-bound slave stares willessly
That only planets charm a star?
O distant star, who wilelessly
Has trapped the mind of tiny man,
Release him from this senseless grip
That draws him to the airless main
Where everlasting sleeps do drift.

CREATION

She made herself
out of pale lipstick
gypsy shawl
peasant blouse
added lace
stitching memories
latticing pleasantly;
naïve shoes
worn to fit
remembering country dances

THE SEARCH

I went a-searching through my dreams
Down fragrances, along thought streams —
In mists, cold echoes clop-clopped, while soft shoe
Through broken cobwebs rainbowed dew.

DANCERS

Dinosaurs dance sedately.
Because of their weight and their delicate toes.
Their walnut-sized brains and their clattering clothes,
Dinosaurs dance sedately.

BUT dreamers all dance in their minds.
Because of perhapsing and pop-corny hope,
And inside-out thoughts of incredible scope,
Dreamers all dance in their minds.

When will YOU join the dance?
Oh, that's what the earth's for —
A wild ballroom-dance floor
So when will you join the dance?
PLEASE — say you will join the dance!

THE BEAUTIFUL WORDS

Sometimes I stand at the door of a dark night
and whistle,
and the beautiful words come running.
Then times come for the empty search
of well-trod ground
of dank hollow wells
where I cannot find a sound,
oh — except these
tool words
someone left lying
in a broken box.

INQUIRY

"What is love, oh, what is love?" she cried,
"A feeling gentle toward the one you love?
A feeling strong to ward off stings for him?
A feeling safe through all his flick'ring moods?
A feeling free while in his prisoning palm?
Oh tell me, for I do not know of love."

MYSTERY

Like the prisms of an opal,
Never changing nor the same —
Living paradox in heart-fall —
I hate, I like — yet you remain.

Like a shimm'ring violin-song
Lost to ear but truly kept,
Seeming gone, but never quite gone —
Whom of you shall I accept?

TRACES

No stone will ever show
        how lightly dance his feet
Nor reflect how sweet
        his laughter as it bells
                        in my ears
        No clever statue catch
            his warming smile!
And though I may try to
write of him, look through the
hollows between the words & reality
        & see as much

WORDS

I thought we were talking side by side
Didn't know you were in front
Taking my words on the chin
       — words never meant to hurt
       — never meant to bruise
       — words meant to walk side by side with yours
And in the evening afterglow,
In the early fireplace light
You quietly crying
And I didn't know . . .

SLEEPING OFF THE COLD MORNING

Sleeping off the cold morning
In a warm woolly blanket and the arms of my love,
Planning in a dreamy way
What we will do in the warm noon-day . . .
      Eden in a fragile night
      Adam in the first sunlight
      Paradise with thee, my love —
      Downy quilt and stars above . . .

Sleeping in and dreaming in the dawn —
Kiss me now before I wake.
Share with me the still day-break
      When the herald birds are hushed . . .

      In the arms of my love —
      In the arms of my love, planning
What we shall do in the warm noon-day.

TWO CANDLES BURNING

Two candles burning, dispelling the night —
Where does one flame end?
Wick, wax, and fire blend
Into one light.

See the light, sweet and warm, where there were two?
Mingling and melting,
Soaring and lilting,
Dancing life through.

THE CARD

It's just posterboard and ink
  and a verse thousands read and think
    "Just right!"
They've bought and sent,
  seeing the people they love
  or through duty would honor
  or some barely known to surprise with print —
  or people they hate!
        but hate more giving cause
        to feel superior and berate
        this most brusque purchaser of my card!

My card — I see you handling it —
Your hands cup it —
It's cupped in your hands
  Like a candle flame you would guard
And you smile over its edge
Touched by the well-wrought words
  of the clever well-paid wordsmith
  and the visions once more well-expressed
      in colored ink —
         landscapes,
         still lifes,
         improbable cats, bears,
            dogs or mice —

But on this bit of posterboard — this fragile craft —
  so easy to misconstrue
  rides a trembling heart
    from me to you.

GIFT CARD

They're dancing around in the cage of my mind,
The words and their twins writ for you to find!
Anniversary, birthday, Christmas — all share
The occasional chance to say that I care.

MAY ALL YOUR SWAINS

"May all your swains
As you pass by
Sigh with pity
For th' eddying breeze
Bereft of such a
       Pretty!"

OH DEAR

I'm not at all what I used to be —
Has anyone seen where I left me?
The glass reflects the passing shell;
The ruins of Troy lie where they fell.
Leave powdered Helen in a heap?
or shall I sweep?

THE STAR-TRIMMED MUG; MADE IN CHINA

Fingers not quite
      colored white,
Number: five
      built to survive,
Gently shaped
      this smooth blue brink
      from which I drink.

Her heav'n like mine wears stars
She's loved both Moon and Mars
      with eyes like mine,
And we divine
Shared joy:
This toy.

SORTING SCREWS

Delicious
Absorbing —
Simple work — finding, filling
      patterns
How are you going to do this?
I don't know.
Let me do it awhile
then I will tell you
How.
If you've tasted the trance
It will flash in your glance.

MYSTERY

Don't you just hate when you clean out a drawer
And not all things fit that fit before!

THE PERFECT PLACE

I always feel successful when I've just cleaned up my space —
A box or niche for everything and each is in its place.

And yet I know two weeks from now there'll be an anguished howl —
We've got to find that paper's clever newly-hidden file!

THE TRAIN AND TROLLEY PILE

It is our music!
How it fills our house —
Tread with ginger feet
Our many-mansional paper jungle —
My enemy and my friend the paper moat
       obsequious
       encroaching
       undercrunching
       web words knitting us
       to tons of metal sliding screeching people boxes —
Footprints crackle — this is our home;
                     this is its anthem —
       our litanies' appoggiatura
       of shaved-wood surf — our music.

VIRTUAL MATE
(The Computer Widow's Lament)
(or Computer After-laughter)

I wonder
        (If he dies)
Can I have an outstanding
        understanding
With a taxidermist specialist
        (a standing underwritten
        special outing—via taxi,
        natur'lly)
Actually to convey him thither
        — and back
And sit him up so straight
        — (the Late)
— he is so straight a sitter
Entranced, enhanced, advanced
        finger on mouse,
Eyes glazed, gaze hazed
        but just a little —
So life-like
        (just don't banter —
        he won't answer —)
He'll look so wise
In such disguise

SUPPER WILL BE LATE

Stand Still Time!
Parade Rest petulant my demand!

Can't you see
      I've a new book of poems in hand
Insistent entreaties
      luring rhyme drumbeats
           to new opened doors
I've entered thought through your gates
      and my feet are happily
bemired in a Stranger's river
of words

The Lute in my heart
      still reverberates with
         his songs
It's Stand Still Time
. . .
O, supper will be late.

CHILDSONG

They're keeping the sun just over the hill
But no matter how fast we ride
He's gone to bed
(My mother has said)
When we get to the other side.

The drive is long and so is our song,
The verses get mixed in my head —
I plan to say reams
But they turn to dreams
Woven of quicksilver thread.

HUSH

Hush! Hush!
"Hush-Hush-Hush"
Brushes his teeth with a vegetable brush
Walks all night on a mountain of mush
Tickles small owls till they sing like a thrush —
That's Baby's night-friend,
"Hush-Hush-Hush"!

THE SKUNK

It's hard to be cross at a skunk —
She can't help she got scared and stunk.
She sprinkled the breezes
With defensive sneezes
And it's better'n a bitten-out chunk!

EASTER HOUSE

Two china rabbits, out again,
　fix soft-eyed stares like wonder
　(day night day night day night day)
　and see no miracle embodied large in th'candle-wax smooth pink
　　　　and very perfect Egg betwixt.

Meanwhile mid-window parade past latches
　drake, duck, duckling, smallest duck
　(predestined to devotion man and maiden may much envy)
　drenched in brilliant dawn.

Yet only hearts in human clay will ever see the hallowing light,
　so different from the mundane ray our little star pours out
　　　　erasing night.

THANKSGIVING

Thanksgiving evening, around the cleared table
Brains strain
for the game,
   cards a-blur —
While the lovely lilting
   river of familiar voices
   passes over me and
   I drown, not caring,
For I'm finding the dream stream
         of voices from other
         feasts floating by,
         smiles left in my mind
               by dear faces long gone,
         A sunset of sweet music left in my ears alone,
         visions of dining rooms
               in houses long since sold, changed, charming yet.
               I roam them so often
         my inner glance caressing, happy.
Meanwhile this fantasy NOW
      is playing along like a TV
someone forgot to turn off.

THE BUS

The important roar and snort of a bus,
The impatient way it sighs at the light,
The way it ignores the car-sized fuss,
The flash of its sides in a light at night:

These make me ignore the gasoline smell;
The troubles of the tedious ride.
These hold a certain "Return!" smell
That changes like the sea's own tide.

COAL

Will no one love the coal-banks now?
Piles of dullness shift (coal) these
Glacial floes of jetsam (coal), newly
Cracked from manless slough (coal).

Red-sweatered second grader thuds
His mighty plaything (coal), does not see
Dirty beauty — long-dead death (coal),
Starving out its thief.

Hope and ache and will chip through
Black strength (coal), under-earth.
Blood, bones, forests (coal), man-unthought,
Save as memorial mountained COAL.

She (that cleans house hates
Griminess (coal); shifting grit)
Shakes thin fist, can't rouse
Post-pain stupor of black heat.

WE CANNOT SHAKE ITS
        GIANT SLUMBER.

LIFESTREAM

The piping flute
Her dream
His cello counterpoint
Knowing pipes
And plumb —
Rankering tax
Singers swell in chorus
A cricket frenzy
Round on round
With piteous
Ensamples
Dreaded dreadful

Government
We
Swayed as grasses
In riptide

Rooted in old rope
The middle —
Where most people
Live in hope
Cry and love
And
Sift and vote!

ABSURD

"Absurd!" —
What a wonderful word!
A laugh that bursts
Like water balloons.
Drenched we are —
We've been buffoons! —
Shoring up crazy-quilt
Government guilt,
      prettily pricking,
      pettily picking . . .
Don't point your finger at me "Kew-Kew"
Or I will see They jail You-You!

AN INSINUATION

("Murderer!")

In the cry-scream of a child's despair.
'Turned with helpless wrath and hopeless groan—
Earth to warn — An anthology alone
Bearing Caesar to an empty square.

("Murderer!")

Trade winds of a friendship Beauty bore
Streaking to an haven walled with fjords,
Safe from Hatred's high-held wooden swords.
Then the sneered suggestion — nothing more.

("Murderer!")

Static-words struck unexpected pain.
Beauty's twisted smile; Her tears, so rare —
Then 'twould poison Him with death-dark stare
But I stab poor Beauty, hating Cain!

CHIMERA

                           — just there
Between river and road —
No, no! To the left of that rock!

An invisible line
A century ago
        — some fought to move
        — more died to save
That line you can't see —

                           — just there
Between river and road —
No, no! To the left of that rock!

Later scholars will quarrel, ask where,
None living will know
Nor anyone care —
        No, no one will . . . care.

SHORT POEMS

work rhythm gets going and you hate
to stop even though you ache . . .
you're "in the swing"

Dismayed by sudden visions
of what was wrong with what
we were doing

Any requests, Lord? Anything
You'd like me to sing?

To the God who thought it would
be a nice touch to grace our days
with laughter

Defuse the ticking bombs
of nurtured hate

☼

My cup is full of memories,
and only some are sweet

☼

with her feelings all
boarded up against
the gray sky day

☼

a song I thought I'd
never remember
goes dancing
through my mind

☼

singing with
mosquito per-
sistence

☼

Sometimes mind goes
round like idle wheel
of bike tied to a car

STOP TO THINK

Where does this running get one?
      this running without a pause,

Nowhere unless you are running
      for a good and a worthy cause.

The world hastens on for a dead-end
      in this highly commercialized age,

A business man running his circuit
      is like a fox in a tread-mill cage.

"YOU DON'T KNOW ME, BUT - -"

Somebody somewhere is looking to you,
Not for clothing or food or brick clay,
But he really is looking you through and through,
For he's building his life on your Way.

ON THE SUBWAY

I saw them on a subway
Fling into seats
Ears plugged with radio,
Eyes slid out of focus.
One line crimped a forehead
(would not leave a trace —
such dewy skin!)
I cannot speak —
("Don't talk to strangers—"
Having mothers, we both know!)
Yet I ache to ask —
"Tomorrow Man,
what do you hear?
That line — a trace
of hate words
Trampolining in your ears?
Or puzzle-tracked
philosophies to stitch
your memories to life with
Threads of human hope?"
Forgivably, humbly, to the dear God above
I pray you hear
Love.

RENA'S READING OF SWEET "PSALM 16"

I.

I said to Him:
> You are my Lord; I have no other help but yours.
> I want the company of those who love you —
> > they are the true nobility.

Those choosing other gods shall be filled with
> sorrow; I will not offer the sacrifices they
> do, or even speak the names of their gods.

The Lord Himself is my inheritance, my prize,
> my food and drink; my highest joy.

He guards all that is mine . . . I will fall heir to pleasant brooks
and meadows.

I will bless the Lord Who counsels me; He
> gives me wisdom in the night.
> He tells me what to do.

I am always thinking of Him, and because He is
> so near I never need stumble or fall —
Heart, body and soul are filled with joy.

Lord,
> You will not leave me among dead men.

> > You let me feel the joys of Life, the exquisite
> > pleasure of Your own eternal Presence.

Save me, dear God — I have come to you
for refuge.

II.

I said to Him,
        You are my Lord, I have no other help.
        I would mingle with your followers
                        here and now.

Those choosing hollow gods shall reap sorrow —
Your good gifts I will not give up to please
Idols whose names shall not even pollute
        my mouth.

You Yourself are my inheritance, my
        high prize, my food, my drink; my
        highest joy
                You have set my boundaries and
                I see it is good.

I would call down blessings upon you,
a Source of Blessings. In prayers
and dreams You bring me wisdom
in the night. I wake up knowing what to do.

WE SEEK HERE

We seek here the wild and Living Stream
That bright river that gladdens the City of God!
We desire the clear refreshing Stream
such as Moses unleashed with the lash of his rod —
Somewhere it flows!
Somewhere it flows!
Somewhere it flows!

Faint it chimes through our dark forest — days.
How it sparkles with reason, it dances with hope,
glints between tall stony grating days.
But we thrill to its thunder and gasp at its scope,
Somewhere it flows!
Somewhere it flows!
Somewhere it flows!

Pilgrim, cool your face at this Sweet Spring!
Drench yourself, safely lost in God's will to revive!
Quest to share! This is the Living Spring,
more abundantly blessing as share it we strive.
This Jesus knows!
This Jesus knows!
This Jesus knows!

THE SEARCH

I searched for my best Friend today.
With glad heart I started to look.
The calendar said it was Sunday,
"Worship day," claimed the Good Book.

I entered the wealthy cathedral
And sat on its polished pew.
I waited to find God Eternal
But He'd left there, so I did, too.

I went to the movie that same day,
I eagerly followed the plot.
I hoped I would find Him in that way —
It passed and I missed Him a lot.

Now a small church I entered.
The people were hostile and cold.
All seemed to be quite self-centered
And prejudice had taken hold.

I left the hot city to stroll on
Through country untraveled and wild.
Before the sun was quite gone
Came the Presence so gentle and mild.

I searched for my best Friend today.
With glad heart I started to look.
I couldn't find Him on Broadway.
Instead, in a wooded nook.

HE'S THERE

Green and tranquil the forest stands,
Calm forgotten wooded strands.
Rambling paths for troubled minds,
Where the soul communion finds.

Something strong is in the wood,
Something strange, but something good.
Now I know what this thing is,
I walk with Christ, my hand in His.

Twilight creeps on to invade,
Where the sunset's bright rays fade.
Slow am I to leave this church
Made by God of oak and birch.

CAMPUS — 5:15 P.M.

Ring, Angelus. Do not tell
A skeptic called a chaplain
Sits beneath you

Death
Real death

I am not afraid; I knew the
Suffocation of his Lazarus-gaze —
"Doubt for the sake of doubt"

Praise be to God!
There was a man
From Thailand
Who left with me (back to dorms, Thursday)

His brown face smiled and there was God
He said, "It works.
Christianity works when all
The words are done and I
Walk out to live."

SPRING BREAKS

Not in the first race of
   chipmunk strife
Nor in the startled crocii's
   pastels palette rife
Nor thrilling trill of
   lark and wren accord —

But in the Spring
   of my beloved Lord
   out of the ground —
   Heavenbound —

Blazing the Way
   for my rejoicing soul
   to rise above —
   Awash in Love

EPIPHANY

God speaks. Listen — this has worth
See the wild display —
Fire unfurls to carpet Earth
white tempests round Him play

PLEA

Caught in the act
Between being and becoming
Frozen by the flash of Thy
Lightning . . .
Defenseless as wild animals
alarmed . . .
O, judge most mercifully Lord!

KAIROS

She stands in life without sight of it.
Eyes of her fix with watching.
She looks for Kairos.
She must be ready —
For Kairos.

She moves through life without touch of it.
Hands of her stiffen from stillness.
She waits for Kairos.
She must be ready —
For Kairos.

She strides past life without heed for it.
Ears of her ache for ultrasonics.
She listens for Kairos.
She must be ready —
For Kairos.

She reaches death without living.
Kairos in life has been none of her.
She leaves Chronos.
She must be ready —
Kairos.

JUNGLE

Jungles of danger lie around

She is as a blind person
Set about with quicksand.
— Nowhere safe to turn
— No hand true to grasp
— No voice clear to guide
Through the invisible
        Jungle.

And turning, she frets
tries
        steps
                is sure

                        falls.

IDYLL

Uninspired inspiration!
    This I have waited.
    This I have fought.
        The ticking of a clock?
        The singing of a lamp?

        The peace of her sleep?
Yes. The peace of her sleep,
    And the sturdy friendship . . .
        the trust — vulnerable —
    And the peace —
        the peace of her sleep.

Quiverless and full, her sleep . . .
    A mist that laps around my
        wakefulness . . .
    An ether without panic.
    Life tolerating death.

I have a trust, a faith . . .
I too, shall sleep
      . . . perhaps, more soundly . . .

CHOICE

Pray naught else be like regret!
Such unholy grief —
Thoughts which should have died squirm free.
Decision idly lacerates
The mind that struck and tempered it —
The other way — the other chance — the haunting
Why oh why oh why — ever!

Shun hope and suck in scream
Poor blind . . .

                    Perhaps a dream will hear . . .

LATE

Soft I've padded well past midnight.
Now I wade against the unseen current
  of the River Lethe that floods my living room
        flowing invisible around me
        and I've breathed its ethers

Oh, just a paragraph — a small one —
        this letter's nearly done.
I know the words, have spelt them
        since 3rd Grade!
Yet now rebel fingers have drawn "M"
        where I said "W"!
And how did "p" get there,
        trolling below the line in place of the "b"
        I ordered a scant minute ago!

Once more I floss, staring mindless
  at the bright-voiced newscaster
  who's been struggling to gain my attention,
  all peppermint perkiness, as though understanding
  it will be a steep climb — these glass trails
  of my neuron's paths connecting their way down
        to the Miracle of Sleep.

THE GOOD SAFE PLACE

I remember just yesterday I thought
I must put that in a
      Good Safe Place.

Now where was that
      Good Safe Place!

After searching long & hard
      for the good safe place

I've begun to wonder
      what it was I'd thought
          I'd put in such
              a good safe place.
Ah well — at least it's in a good safe place.

Some future
      archaeologist will take a
fine bristled brush and find the little treasure and
      the wondering
         will live on.

SUDDEN FRIGHT

Too long in one place
Like a tree
I play Russian Roulette
With the spinning world.
My refugee mind
Plans to flee,
Tracks the solitaire Moon
through the fingering clouds
Flying free.

CONCENTRATION

One step at a time,
one step at a time.
Lord keep my mind
on what I'm
doing one step
at a time!

POEM TO OLD WRITINGS

How good to be tired,
Tired
And sit in sun and know
From writings
What I was and felt

Howdo, me.
Why, much forgot is worth
Regathering
I shall be that of me
Again! I shall be me.

No longer old & rut-deep
Riding same and known —
No more!

Thank God there're parts of
me (& thee as well) I do not
always know.
        And now consign my
tired-out self to be forgot
        And dug up after rains.

NOTES ON THE POEMS

The Early Poems were collected in a book titled Just Poems by Ethelrene Johnson in 1955.

All of Rena's poems were first hand-published and hardbound by Fred Gerhard with Rena's permission and proofreading for *Poetry by Rena Gerhard*, published in 2005, which included her introduction excerpted here.

"Absurd" was written at Electric City Trolley Museum May 12, 2002 (Mother's Day) and published in *Musings* August 11, 2002.

"Accepting Peace" was published in *Musings* in the Fall of 1990.

"An Insinuation" was written February 10 – 17, 1955. The reference in it is to Mark Antony in Shakespeare's "Julius Caesar".

"Campus-5:15 p.m." was written as a reaction to an atheist who was an official chaplain at Penn State University, and bears the note at the bottom of the page, "How does the Devil manage to do this?"

"Childsong" was published in *Musings* on September 17, 2000.

"Choice" was written as the ninth poem of ten assignments in the spring semester of 1955.

"Creation" was published in *Musings* October 18, 1987.

"Dancers" was written for children.

"Earth-Cry" is from December, 1954.

"Earth-Cry (II)" is from February 17 – 24, 1955. This poem is a reworking of the first version (above) to meet the requirements of a Penn State Poetry Composition class that taught: "Today we don't write such form-following poetry" as Sonnets, which I think it was.

"Easter House" was written March 24, 2001.

"Hush" was written for children.

"Idyll" was the seventh poem of ten assignments from spring of 1955.

"Inquiry" was written January, 1955.

"Kairos": kairos – A time when conditions are right for the accomplishment of a crucial action; the opportune and decisive moment – *Webster's 3rd New International Dictionary Unabridged* (1966).

"Lifestream" was published in *Musings* April 1, 1990.

"May all your swains" was written for my granddaughter January 30, 2002.

"Mystery" was written January, 1954.

"Night Walk" was published in *Musings* November 12, 1995.

"Oh Dear" was published in *Musings* March 25, 1990.

"Perception" is from March, 1954.

"Sleeping Off the Cold Morning" are lyrics for a song given to Fred and Rachael Gerhard.

"Spring Breaks" was written for Easter cards March 25, 2002.

"Thanksgiving" was written late fall, 2003.

"The Perfect Place" was submitted to *The Reading Eagle* September 10, 1999.

"The Waves" was completed April 2005.

"This Snow" was written mid-January 2003.

"Traces" was written April 14, 2005.

"Two Candles Burning" are lyrics written for Fred and Rachael Gerhard's wedding, and was sung by Fred and Rachael at their wedding reception.

"Virtual Mate" was written March 21, 1998.

"You Don't Know Me, But--" was written in the summer of 1953.

ACKNOWLEDGEMENTS

Many of these poems were originally published in *Musings,* the poetry column of *The Reading Eagle,* including "Absurd," "Accepting Peace," "Childsong," "Creation," "Lifestream," "Night Walk," and "Oh Dear." And "Dancers" was featured on *Bespoke Vocals* on YouTube, read by the actor Kirk Lawrence-Howard. Deep gratitude to J. Calvin Gerhard for permission to publish Rena's work.

ABOUT THE AUTHOR

Rena Gerhard's poems were published frequently in *Musings (The Reading Eagle).* She also had her poetry featured in an episode of *Bespoke Vocals* read by the actor Kirk Lawrence-Howard. She started writing at an early age, and for nearly 60 years. She received her bachelors degree in English from Penn State University where she went on to earn a masters degree in Philosophy. She did work towards a doctorate in English at Penn State, and taught Logic at the Penn State Campus in Altoona, PA. A composer of hymns and counterpoint pieces, she also enjoyed folk dancing, ballroom dancing, and in her youth, ballet. She lived in Pennsylvania with her husband and sons primarily as a homemaker, dance instructor, and Sunday school teacher. Rena frequently expressed her joy in family life, and in a love of Jesus and God. She was an inspiration to others to follow their creative endeavors fully, to make music, sing, dance — and yes — to write poetry.

www.ingramcontent.com/pod-product-compliance
Lightning Source LLC
Chambersburg PA
CBHW010939120626
46554CB00008B/2543